Ivy Hall School
1072 Ivy Hall Lane
Buffalo Grove, IL 60089

The Let's Talk Library

Let's Talk About When You Have to Have Your Appendix Out

Melanie Ann Apel

The Rosen Publishing Group's
PowerKids Press™
New York

To my Michael and all others with tummy troubles. Thank you for understanding mine, too.

Published in 2002 by Rosen Publishing Group, Inc.
29 East 21st Street, New York, NY 10010

First Edition

Book Design: Colin Dizengoff
Project Editors: Jennifer Landau, Jason Moring, Jennifer Quasha

Photo Credits: pp. 4, 12 © Custom Medical; pp. 11, 16, 19, 20 © Index Stock; pp. 7, 8 © CORBIS; p. 15 © Cindy Reiman.

Apel, Melanie Ann.
Let's talk about when you have to have your appendix out / Melanie Ann Apel.— 1st ed.
   p. cm. — (The let's talk about library)
Includes bibliographical references and index.
   ISBN 0-8239-5865-5 (library binding)
1. Appendix (Anatomy)—Juvenile literature. 2. Appendicitis—Juvenile literature. 3. Appendectomy—Juvenile literature. [1. Appendix (Anatomy) 2. Appendicitis. 3. Diseases. 4. Appendectomy.]
[DNLM: 1. Appendectomy—Child—Juvenile literature. WI 535 A641L 2002] I. Title. II. Series.
   RD542 .A64 2002
   617.5'545-dc21
                                                                          2001000151

Manufactured in the United States of America

Contents

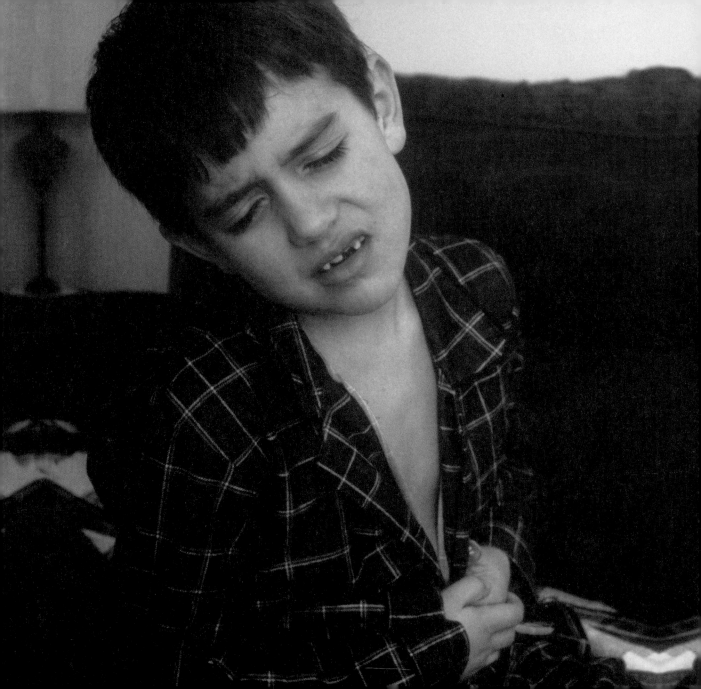

Michael's Stomachache

Michael's stomach aches. It aches so much that he can't concentrate on his homework. Michael tells his mom. She puts Michael to bed and gently rubs his belly. He still feels awful. Michael starts to feel **nauseous**, too.

"It really hurts!" Michael cries. When he stands up and walks to the bathroom, his stomach hurts even more. He throws up. Michael's mom knows it is time to call the doctor. Michael's mother is not sure what is wrong with her son, but she worries that the problem may be his appendix.

If your stomach hurts a lot, your mother or father will call the doctor. Your appendix might be the problem.

What Is an Appendix?

Everyone has an appendix. Your appendix is an **internal organ**. An organ is a group of cells. Internal means that it is inside your body. Most organs do important and special jobs. Your appendix is a small, thin tube that looks like a finger. It is connected to your **large intestine**. Your appendix sits in the lower right side of your stomach. Doctors and scientists do not know why a person has an appendix or what function this organ serves in the body.

Doctors and scientists don't know why people have an appendix or what it is meant to do. ▶

Appendicitis

When your appendix suddenly becomes **inflamed**, it means that it is red and swollen and it hurts very much. This is called **appendicitis**. Appendicitis often starts with pain around the belly button. Your tummy will hurt when you move or walk. Nausea, **vomiting**, fever, and stomach pain are the four main signs of appendicitis. Your pain probably will be mostly in your lower right side. One way to tell if you have appendicitis is to press the right side of your belly and hold it. Let it go fast. If that hurts, it may be appendicitis.

◀ *When you have appendicitis, you don't feel like eating.*

Who Gets Appendicitis?

Most people who get appendicitis are older teenagers or people in their early twenties. However, some kids and older adults get appendicitis, too. There's no way to control whether you get appendicitis or not. If appendicitis is taken care of right away, you should have a quick and full recovery. Appendicitis is one of the most common reasons why kids have emergency surgery. About 4 out of every 1,000 kids have an **appendectomy** each year. You might know a kid who has had his or her appendix out.

You can't control whether or not you get appendicitis, but you can make sure it is taken care of right away. ▶

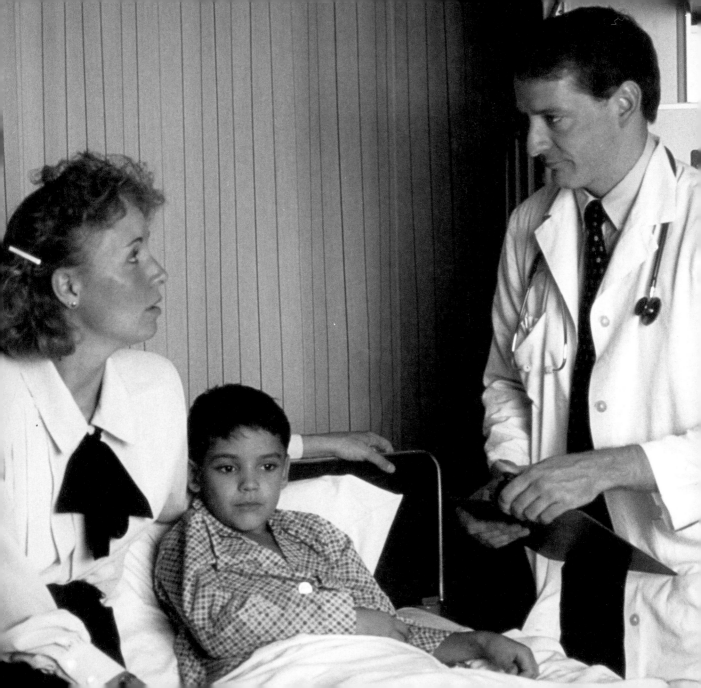

Before the Operation

The only way to cure appendicitis is by removing the appendix. Most likely, you will have to go to the hospital for an operation. Your doctor might want to do a few tests before the operation. At the hospital, you will change out of your clothes and into a special hospital gown. After you lie down on a bed, your doctor will give you medicine called **anesthesia**. Anesthesia helps you sleep through the operation. While you are asleep, you will not feel any pain. When the operation is over, the anesthesia will wear off and you will wake up.

Your doctor gives you anesthesia to help you sleep through an operation. When it wears off, you wake up.

13

Getting Your Appendix Out

During the operation, your doctor will make a small, deep cut in your belly. Your doctor will remove your appendix through this cut. After your appendix is removed, the doctor will close up the cut. When you wake up, you will have a bandage over the cut on your belly. Later, after your skin heals from your operation, you will have a small **scar** on your belly. The scar will remind you that you had your appendix taken out.

The small scar on your belly will remind you of your operation. ▶

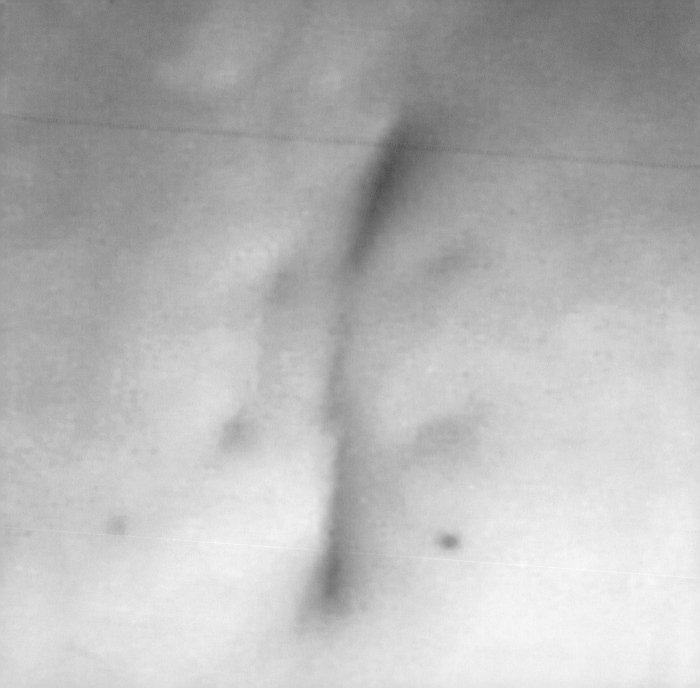

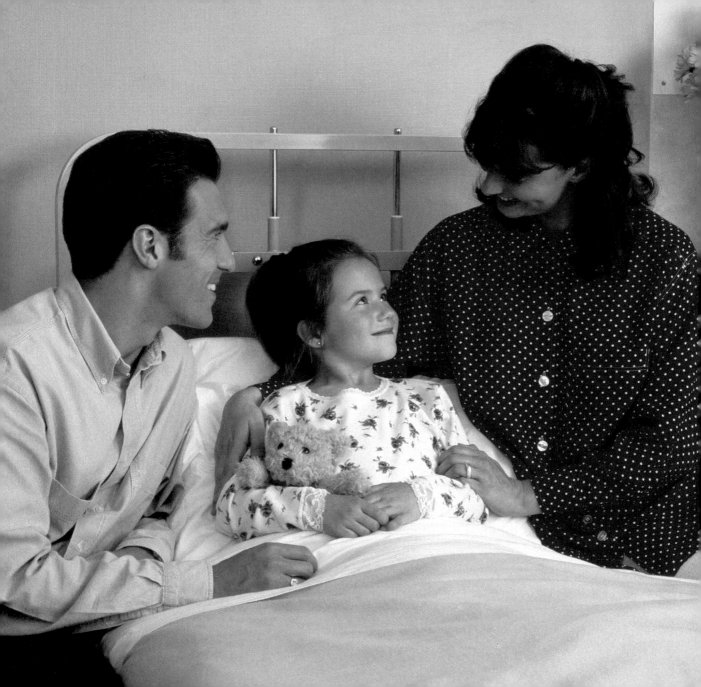

You Won't Be Alone

Your mom, dad, or someone you love will be waiting for you when you wake up after your operation. You won't be alone. Your favorite stuffed animal or blanket may be there. Your belly will feel sore for a few days. You may feel tired from being sick. Nurses and doctors will take care of you while you are in the hospital. Also, you can have visitors while you get better. Visitors may bring you special gifts and treats to enjoy!

It can be scary to have an operation, but you should remember that you are not alone.

A Ruptured Appendix

If appendicitis is not treated, an inflamed appendix can burst. This is called a **ruptured** appendix. A ruptured appendix can be dangerous. Doctors always want to take out an appendix that might burst. Sometimes an appendix does rupture, or burst. People who have a ruptured appendix need to have their appendix taken out right away. Whether you have appendicitis or a ruptured appendix, if it is taken care of properly you will have a full recovery.

If you have a ruptured appendix removed right away, you should be able to leave the hospital before long. ▶

Recovering from the Operation

After your appendix operation, you might not want to eat big meals or drink a lot. The nurse will give you sips of liquid, Popsicles, and Jell-O. In a few days, you will want to eat regular food. Soon you will feel well enough to go home. Even at home, you should rest for a while. You shouldn't play sports or lift heavy things. It's important to take good care of yourself because your body needs time to heal. Read, nap, and talk to your family and friends about what you want to do when you are all better!

◀ *Make sure to get plenty of rest after your operation. Soon you will be able to do all of your favorite things again.*

Out of School

   You probably will miss some days at school when you have your appendix taken out. Don't worry. Your parents will let your teacher know that you won't be there. What you have to do is just as important as school. Having your appendix taken out can be scary, but if you take care of yourself, you soon will feel well again. While you're out of school, your teacher might even send you some homework so that you don't fall behind. Take time to heal and soon you will be back at school with all of your friends.

Glossary

anesthesia (a-nus-THEE-zhuh) Medicine that makes you sleep so that you do not feel pain.

appendectomy (a-pen-DEK-tuh-mee) Removal of the appendix.

appendicitis (uh-pen-duh-SY-tis) A sickness when your appendix suddenly becomes inflamed.

inflamed (in-FLAYMD) Something that is red and swollen and hurts very much.

internal organ (in-TER-nuhl OR-gun) An organ inside your body.

large intestine (LARJ in-TES-tin) The wide, lower part of the intestines where water is absorbed from waste and waste gets ready to move out of your body.

nauseous (NAW-shus) Feeling like you are going to throw up.

ruptured (RUP-sherd) Burst.

scar (SKAR) A mark on your skin that reminds you that the skin there once was cut.

vomiting (VAH-mit-ing) Throwing up.

Index

Ivy Hall School
10772 Ivy Hall Lane
Buffalo Grove, IL 60089